The Inner Compass

Success Stories of Massachusetts Foster Children

Carol Yelverton, Editor

To order additional copies of this book, contact:
Xlibris Corporation
1-888-7-XLIBRIS
www.Xlibris.com
Orders@Xlibris.com

Contents

THIS BOOK IS DEDICATED TO ALL CHILDREN WHO HAVE SUFFERED FROM NEGLECT AND ABUSE, IN THE HOPE THAT THESE STORIES HELP TO PROVIDE SAFETY, STRENGTH AND PEACE.

Introduction

Home and family are as basic to most people as breathing. Family is the place we come from. It is the place where we first know love. It is, by nature, filled with ups and downs. Yet, whatever our circumstances, it is our center. It is a personal defining point.

Yet, what happens if a family breaks down? Children and teenagers sometimes have to enter foster care if they cannot be safe at home. It is traumatic and life changing for those who find themselves removed from their families because of abuse or neglect. Even if one is relieved to get away from the problems for a while, the reality of leaving parents and home can be shattering. It is a time when many young people feel a great deal of pain and confusion about what to do next.

There are those, though, who have come before. Many foster children have not only made it through this difficult period of time in their lives; they have actually ended up living out their very own success stories. In their own words, this book chronicles the lives of some of these courageous young people. Their stories are inspirational, not only for other foster children, but for us all. These remarkable people, both current and former foster children, have agreed to share their stories so that others might benefit from their experiences.

This project began in my head one Sunday afternoon, as I wondered what more could be done to help our kids, as they left abuse and neglect behind them. How does one begin to cope with this, or to put the pieces together to make the best of a bad situation?

The insights of those who had already walked this path could offer so much. Many other foster children have had similar experiences within their families. They, too, understand the ache of being uprooted from the only place they knew to be home. Many have inhabited the depths of anger, despair and fear . . . and yet, they've made it out.

This book became a fabulous opportunity to pass along the tools, often developed through trial and error, which could boost self-esteem and help our kids find a positive direction.

Each life story is unique. You may be horrified at the way some of these children have been treated. You should be. They have triumphed over a range of destructive and unspeakable evil. They are truly our heroes.

As individual as each story is, I was struck by how consistently the same elements fell into place to turn around a bad outcome. Over and over, these young people made clear, strong choices for themselves. Each reached a point of being able to take charge of his/her own direction.

For many of us, life often seems like a series of

paths. We know how confusing it can be to choose the way that seems "best" or "right." Somehow, an inner compass surfaced within each of the foster children in this book, signaling the way. There were times when it took a while for the compass to settle down and point a child on, in that direction. Other kids have just always known what was best for themselves. Each person has had his or her own time.

The ability to listen to this internal sense of direction seemed to occur when a child or teen reached a point of selfhood – a belief in and value of one's own self. That's when these foster children showed tremendous courage by setting off on the way that seemed to offer the most good.

The more foster children I encountered, the more grateful I became that I could read and listen to these stories. It truly humbled me to hear each person's truths, and to grasp what it took to push on to the path of higher ground. Although these lives are filled with the experiences of youth, there's a wisdom beyond years in each storyteller's perspective. Some people have chosen to use their actual names. Others have not.

These teens and young adults have received a great deal of help along the way. You'll see what some amazingly committed social workers, foster parents and Adolescent Outreach Workers have done to help each soul rise above the darkness of circumstance. These are their stories, too.

We are using the proceeds of this book to benefit the DSS Kids Fund, which supplies a variety of goods and services to foster children, who would otherwise not receive them.

The Chafee Foster Care Independence Program has provided funding so that we can publish these stories and give copies of this book out to foster children currently in care, so that they can have access to these inspirational words. We are very grateful. Thanks, as well, go out to the DSS Public Affairs Unit for the dedication and energy that has gone into this book, and to the people of the Department of Social Services, who make caring for kids their life's work.

It is an honor to give voice to these young lives. These successes become a testimony for us all, as we each strive to hold, strong and clear, to our own inner compass.

Carol Yelverton
Public Affairs Director
The Massachusetts Department of Social Services

Jason

I HAVE TO consider myself very lucky. I didn't
have the worst. There are kids out there who are
beaten and have the worst done to them. I was fortu-
nate. I just had my mother: an alcoholic. She was
bipolar and she didn't get the help she needed. I
didn't have a stable family involved. All my brothers
and sisters were much older. I was left behind, in a
sense. No one really wanted to know how Jason was
doing.

I have lived the life of alcoholism—lies, hiding
and depression—for too long. But, I've had an an-
gel with me the whole way. I was only placed into two
foster homes. A lot of it was hard, but I grew from it.
I'm still growing from it. There's so much now, that I
still have to work through. I think the first part is rec-
ognition and going from there. I grew up in Duxbury,
Massachusetts, a wealthy town . . . "Deluxebury", everyone called it. I lived there until I was eleven. My father was involved in a lot of illegal activities. He made

hundreds of thousands of dollars, but, unfortunately, he was a gambler.

The life he got involved in meant that there was a lot of money he blew away. We're talking two thousand to four thousand dollars a day gambling. Of course, he and my mother had their differences about that. My mother kind of got carried away with spending, too. Then, as my father went to prison, for a year or two, my mother took to alcoholism. She didn't have the picture perfect life. She dreamed of having this home in Duxbury. He ended up going to prison. She found out he was cheating on her. So, she had a lot to deal with all at once. Then she developed lung cancer.

I had to be the stable one for her. It was hard. I saw all these changes taking place in her. I didn't know how to deal with it. All I knew was that she was crying all the time. She had attempted suicide. It wasn't picture perfect. Sometimes money is more evil than good. It was a lot to cope with. I think at that time I didn't realize much. I didn't socialize much. My mother kind of hoarded me. She wanted me there. It made her comfortable. I gave her joy, but it suffocated me. She didn't let me go out and try my wings. I started gaining weight.

By the time I was 10 years old, she had been to detox. My father sold the house. He had to pay back loans. My parents were together on and off. My mother and I moved to Florida with 50 thousand dollars. We came back to Massachusetts several months later with five thousand dollars. Some guys had taken advantage of her. Of course, she was drinking the whole time we were down there, so it doesn't take long. Money is one of the easiest things in the world to get rid of.

We ended up living next door to my father. Then my mother couldn't afford the rent so we ended up going from apartment to apartment. I got involved with DSS and ended up moving out to Fort Leavenworth, Kansas with my brother.

After six months I came back. My mother was getting better, so she said. She thought she was all better, but four months later she was back on the bottle. That's when I knew that things were not going to be what she said they were going to be.

I got tired of it. I got tired of lies. I was gaining weight again. It was the same thing. I wanted to go to the mall. She wouldn't even drive me to the mall. I'd moved around so damn much, I didn't have any friends in the area. It was a struggle. At one point I was so upset that by the end of eighth grade I was ready to drop school.

I called DSS. I had seen a TV show on a kid divorcing his mother. I didn't want to do that but I wanted something. I was placed in a foster home nearby, with a wonderful family there. It was hard, though, because I'd never lived with anyone else besides my family. I'd never shared a room. It was a struggle. I didn't fit in right away and I held to my own opinions. The other kids were going through my things and I wasn't used to this happening.

I learned to love, though. I learned about patience. I was there for 8 months. Then it was time to go back home and live with my mother. We moved to another place. She wasn't getting up. She wasn't working. My father was nearby. He had lost the use of his leg. He hadn't gotten treatment for diabetes and gangrene had set in. He became disabled. My father never worked a real job in his life, anyway. He went on disability. My father's attitude about me was, "I can't help him. What can I do? I'm in this small apartment. He can't stay here with me."

He had money. He was still doing his thing. I had to drag it out of him when I needed money for a coat, for clothes. I got tired of my parents being like that. My mother wasn't functional. I had to do everything. I started working 60 hours a week to pay for my mother's bills. I'd do paper routes, rake lawns. That's the way I'd get by. I had to. She went to the food pantry sometimes. People paid me money for those chores, though. I did pretty well. I bought my own food . . . junk, you know . . . subs, pizzas, cupcakes. That's how I gained my weight.

I'd latch on to other people. I'd try to get out of the house. The worst of the worst was the constant moving around and having to lose a sense of childhood. Not having a family is one of the worst things, and not getting the attention I needed at certain times. I don't regret that it happened because I wouldn't want to be other than who I am right now. Because those things happened to me, it made me stronger.

I didn't have a sense of priority then. Back then it was a key for survival. I had to do what I had to do for survival. I missed a lot of school. I had to clean up the messes, make excuses for her all the time, calling work for her and everything else. She made me do the dirty work—you know—clean after her, after she made the mess. You just did what you had to do.

I had learned to lie with my mother because it was the easiest way to do things when she was drinking. I'd lie to satisfy her. Sometimes when you form a habit, you don't even know it and then it turns into something bad. I've learned that lying is not the best thing. Even if you tell a small lie, people will always be questioning you about everything. I learned people will respect you more if you tell the truth.

Finally I said, "I'm about to enter my junior year

at high school. I'm not going to take this." So I started writing senators and state representatives to get her benefits.

There was one woman who took me under her wing. Her name is Kathy Teahan. She was a State Representative from Abington, MA. She really has gone the extra mile. She found me a good home with a dentist. She'd never been a foster parent. I stayed in her home my junior and most of my senior year. Once I got into foster care, I lost forty pounds or so.

Eventually I left her house. I sometimes regretted it later, but I've always acted on impulse, which can be a bad thing, too. I moved in with this girl, but she ended up being bipolar. I latched onto an unhealthy person right away. I wanted to help her. It made me feel comfortable because it was like my mother, in a sense, maybe subconsciously.

Because this was someone I liked so much, I didn't give her the space she needed, sometimes. I'm a very dramatic person, too. I'll make the smallest thing more dramatic, and that can be overwhelming for a person who has enough of her own problems. So I had to learn not to seek attention so much from other people and to be comfortable with myself.

Today, I still have that problem. It's a reassurance thing. I have to learn to deal with it. I can't go back into my past all the time and blame my mother and my father for all my problems. I recognize that, so I have to change. The key is recognizing your problems and working them out. That will help me. I didn't know being an enabler and an attention seeker and a liar was unhealthy. I've had the same therapist for four years. She's really tough on me, but I recognize my problems now. I know what my weak points are. Now, I just have to work on them.

You deal with your problems. You deal with yourself. So I left my girlfriend's house after a month. DSS gave me money for housing. I stayed with friends until the end of the summer. Then I went to college. I lived in the dorms. Sharing space with kids my own age was still tough. I'm mature in some ways and immature in others. That's something that changes with time. You're never completely healed. You have to pick and choose those cards until you're comfortable with yourself. I'm only nineteen. I have a lot more life to live.

Life continues to change, but it's being happy with yourself. It's finding that within and learning how to be a good person. Someday when I'm an old man, I'll look back on my life and say, "Look, I had all these stages. Look from where I've come." I love being in college. It helps you realize what's out there, what's expected of you.

There's nothing now that will faze me. I have seen so much for nineteen, more than most kids my age. Life can really be cruel. I think the thing that kept me going was myself. I really just hoped for a better life. And I had music . . . my singing.

I began in the seventh grade when I signed up for chorus. It was one of the most enjoyable things I'd ever done. It was a great experience for me. Some teachers took me under their wings. One man, Jerry Sims, gave me a passion for music that I'd never had before and he understood me. He was a great, great teacher.

"Phantom of the Opera" was my first real performance. It was absolutely wonderful. I kept singing through high school and went on to compete. I won some festivals. When I was a senior in high school, I was going to go on to college for a business degree. Then I had a chance to sing the National Anthem at graduation. After I saw people stand and heard the applause and with everyone telling after how terrific it was, I said, "Music is what I have to go in for." I want to be a solo performer, the next Pavarotti. I want to be up there on a stage performing for an audience. That's what gives me the most joy.

This year I've started my own business, singing professionally in concerts and at weddings. I'm still in college. I have to work on my grades. You have to work at certain things.

My mother has passed away. I live with my father now, because he has cancer. He has serious medical issues that need to be taken care of. You have to take it one day at a time.

You've got to make the most of your life. Life can't be about money. I could spend the rest of my life with no money, living in a cardboard box, but if I make a difference with my life, it's worth it. Life should make you want to go on. Life's a mystery.

My faith plays a big role. I've been on my knees. I have my private place that I go to and I talk to God, as I'm talking to you now. Sometimes I cry. I need that. I'm not ashamed to say that. All I need is the strength. Then I have to do my part. After my time on earth is done, my biggest dream is to perform in God's heavenly choir, to be one of the voices that people hear before they die.

But I have to work for that. That's why I work on my voice. I want to bring other people joy.

María

I AM 19 years old. During my childhood, I lived with my single mother and grandmother until I was five years old. These were my happiest times. Then my mother got married to my younger sister's father. We lived with them for three years, but I was miserable because he was abusive. He used to beat us and punish us without a reason. He was mean. But in a strange way, I was actually happy because I had a real family with a father. In another way, I never thought it was right for my mother to let him hit me and hit her. I told her it was better before.

She and my stepfather died when I was eight years old. They were killed in Colombia. It happened in the morning. My father had just bought a new car and wanted to fix it. It happened at 7 o'clock. We were all at home. I was in my pajamas. My father wanted us to go with him to my aunt's house.

My sister was on my mother's lap, but I was in the backseat with my uncle and aunt and her small baby. I think someone knew where we were going down the road. My stepfather had been a policeman and had a lot of enemies. I think I had a feeling something was coming. I said to my mother, "Why don't you let my sister come into the back? She doesn't look too comfortable." So my sister sat in the back with me. When she touched the back seat, it happened. On the road, a blue car came out in front of us, and also five or six motorcycles. They cut us off. The men in the car and on the motorcycles had guns. There was one near each window of the car. I got really scared and threw my sister on the floor of the car and lay on top of her.

My uncle threw himself on top of us. They were shooting and shooting and shooting. It felt like it was fireworks. In one way, I was so innocent, though, that I never thought that something like a shooting was happening. Yet, I knew something big was going on. I knew it was a big change.

After the shooting stopped, I got up. My uncle was still on top of us. My mother wasn't moving. My uncle wasn't moving, but my father was still moving, so I got up. When I did that, I guess, those guys, the shooters, started firing at me. I felt a bullet go past the top of my head. I didn't even know what to do. I forgot about my father. I forgot about everything. I didn't even know what my name was. I got out of the car and could tell my father was still alive. I was trying to do something for him. Cars drove by, but people did not want to stop. They were afraid because they did not know what had happened.

Everything had happened in front of one house. Afterwards a lady came out of the house and told us to come inside and wait for the police. They checked my mother's pulse, but she died. My mother had three bullets in her head. My stepfather died a little later because he had not gotten help in time.

I knew I had to be brave because of my three-year-old sister. She was holding me, just attached to my leg, asking me to explain what happened. I called all these phone numbers, but I didn't even know the right one. Finally I got my grandmother, to tell her what had happened, but I didn't know how to say to her that her daughter and her husband had just been killed. I knew she was sick. I told her to sit down and told her bad guys came and killed them. My grandmother came and got us.

That's the worst experience someone could ever have. At the funeral I looked between two caskets. In one of them was my mother, the woman who gave me life. It is too sad.

My grandmother took care of us. I tried to accept the things I could not change because I wanted to set a good example for my sister, no matter what. My mother once told me that if something should happen, I had to protect my sister. Sometimes I think maybe they knew something was going to happen.

My aunt had come to the US to work and regularly sent money because there was no work to have in Colombia. I wanted to go and visit her and I wanted to see the United States. When I was 15 years old, I decided to go to the US and got a five-year visa. To get a visa in Colombia is like a lottery because not everybody can get it, but I was lucky. My grandmother wanted me to go and have a vacation because I had been having a tough time. I immediately liked the US because it was much more peaceful than Colombia. I was really happy and I couldn't believe I was actually in the United States. I didn't know how to speak English though.

The first two weeks with my aunt were nice, but then we started to have some problems. She and I both have strong tempers because of all the stuff that happened before. We did not get along, and six months later I moved out and stayed with some people I had met here. I talked to my grandmother and told her I wanted to stay in the US and look for a better future. In Colombia, I had no money to attend school and there was also no work. I felt I could make a better future for my sister and grandmother.

For two years I stayed with friends without going to school. I didn't have papers. I was going from place to place, sleeping in a friend's car one night, staying with one another night. Even though I was having a tough time, I knew things would turn out fine. But I felt afraid, too, because I didn't know where I'd be the next night.

When I was seventeen, a friend told me she wanted to help me have a better life, to be able to go to school and have good goals. She told me about DSS. At first I was scared because I thought I would be sent back to Colombia. I met with a social worker at DSS. She was such a beautiful person. I told her my story. We talked about going into foster care. I was afraid of the thought of living with strangers because everything would be so new, with a different culture and different food. Sometimes I couldn't understand what people were saying in English.

I did go into foster care, though. The most difficult time in care came when I moved from one foster home to another. Every time it happened, I felt the same fear. I didn't know what was coming. It was hard to get to know new people. I like to cry too much! Every time I left a home, I'd be crying like I was dying. Some of the foster families were so nice.

We couldn't stay together for different reasons. But one foster mother and I stayed in touch. She's always looking out for the best foster home for me to stay in.

Even though I've stayed in good foster homes, it is hard because I've met a lot of other foster children. We all come through with all kinds of stories and problems. It is hard to have to share a room with people you do not know. Sometimes it's okay, but I'm one of those people who likes to keep things neat and really clean. These girls liked me and stuff. They tried to compromise.

Even though it was hard to go into foster care, this has given me so many opportunities that I never would have had. I never would have been able to go to school. I got a job with the Girl Scouts. I had to start as a volunteer because I was under age and didn't have a Social Security card or working papers. In the Girl Scouts I became friends with my supervisor.

I knew Nancy was a special person and that she would make a difference in my life. I could tell her anything, and whenever I had problems or felt bad, I could always turn to her. Nancy wanted me to come and live with her and got in contact with DSS and became my foster mother. I stayed with her until I left care.

I was able to get my working papers. I really worked hard to make that happen. I needed to prove to myself that I could be independent and make it on my own. So many people have been so good to me . . . my social workers and my other foster mother who looked out for me. They have been great, but the one I'm most grateful to is Nancy. She has been extremely good to me.

Dealing with anger has been hard. I used to keep it to myself and not allow anyone to get near me.

Then I'd take it out on everybody else. It changed because I was surrounded by so many people who were patient. I'd talk to people like Nancy. She knew how to calm me down and help me feel better. I used to get so moody that not everyone could have helped me. She used to say, "You have to set your goals." She kept prodding me, even when I had trouble following through. Making it in this new country, graduating high school and learning English have been real accomplishments.

The experience with DSS really changed my life. I never imagined I would do all the things I have. I am proud of myself. All these experiences have made me grow into a mature person. I'm more confident now, and I'm more responsible because I'm taking things more seriously than before.

Today, I have a full time job, my own apartment, and I'm planning on buying my own car. My dream is to go to college this fall to study Early Childhood Education because I always liked kids and would like to work with them.

The only thing I can say is, no matter how difficult things are in our lives, there is always a light at the end of the tunnel. You will see it sometime. You have to work hard to get there. We have to be aware that there are other people out there who have bigger problems than we have.

God has shown me so much. He has put me in this place that I am now. I want to thank all the people who have helped me to be the person I am today, but most of all, I want to thank God. Even though I had a tough time, I know He was there for me.

Christopher

MY NAME IS Christopher. I have been with the Department of Social Services since I can remember. All I know is I was really little, living with my mother on Cape Cod. I was three. I remember some of the things I had, like a "fishy" blanket. I think it's at my uncle's somewhere. I'd like it to be. It's a really comfortable blanket. I don't actually have anything. I try to travel light. I've moved a lot. I only keep the stuff I really use.

My mother and I moved. I was put into foster care for 18 months. My mother had a broken leg.

At first I was excited about this other family. I got to visit my mom once or twice a week. I missed my mom and wished that I was back in my own bed. I was starting to really like chocolate milk. A lot. Now, I can't drink it. Maybe I drank too much of it. Then I went back with her to a new apartment. We were together for a while. At this point, my mom was okay. Then, I don't remember why, but we were evicted.

I saw my Dad once in a while. He passed away

when I was in kindergarten. He had heart problems, but he was afraid of doctors. My mom never married him. I don't remember reacting to his death, good or bad, maybe because I was young.

I moved into a foster home again. I knew this wasn't my first foster home and I knew I wouldn't be with my mom for a while. My first day there, I explored every nook and cranny and quickly learned what was off limits—their kids' rooms, the basement and the master bedroom. I never saw them, although I did see the basement once when it flooded. It was cluttered. I never really did know what was there until then. They had a big screen TV, but it had terrible resolution, and great video games.

Then my life changed again. My mom went to the hospital. I stayed in foster care for 13 months. I remember my uncle taking me for visits. I was at his house a lot. He and my foster father got along. My uncle would take me to visit my mom on weekends. She was at a woman's shelter, waiting for an apartment. They had a machine downstairs where they had chocolate graham crackers. I ate way too many of those, too. Now I just can't eat them, just like the chocolate milk.

I went to live with my mom at the shelter for a week. Then we moved to an apartment. I stayed with my mom for three years. She came upon a drinking problem and got in trouble with guys. What didn't help any is that she got behind in her rent. Her social security got cut, too.

Sherry, my social worker, came out and took me to my next foster home. That was temporary. Then, I moved into another for three weeks. Then I went into a hospital for a month. They tried different drugs to help me, but they didn't work. Then I went to a children's program for 6 months. They had a level system. I made it to the top quickly and got lots of privileges. It was kind of an annoying time. The kids were younger than me (I was twelve by now). I felt like, "Big Trouble in Little China." I was just too big for the place.

I was becoming sad because I'd been away from my mom for a while. I moved into another program for 7 months. This was for the older kids. I got along with most of the kids. Some had criminal troubles and that's tough. I got through the privilege system quickly again and got off-ground privileges. They suspected that I was depressed.

I did have a lot of self-esteem and did well in school. I went camping and rock-climbing. I was doing new and different things.

Here's my philosophy: Life's a game. What's going to happen is going to happen. You just have to make the best of it. I look back and think I just always thought that even when I was much younger. I just hadn't formed the phrase yet. I'm a day-by-day guy. I don't look back on yesterday. I look at now, at what can be done about things now. I think the key to my succeeding is my wanting to. It's all right there. It's just wanting to.

Eventually I moved into this great huge building. These days were the best, so far. I was at the Boston University School in Granby, MA. Population: cows and a couple of sheep. The school was built in a seminary. There were Catholic priests still living there. The staff was nice. Everyone got along with each other. Some of the best friends I ever had were there.

I was there from 4 p.m. December 4, 1998 to June 30, 2000, when the school closed. I still know the exact time and seconds that I left. The friars are still there, as well as the cook. I still go visit them.

Then, I came to my current foster home. I got my first job, as a cashier. Currently, I'm a sophomore in high school with a B average, but I got an A- in biology. I really, really hate Spanish.

I've fallen in love with computers. I plan to become a computer programmer. I want my house to be one where I have three rooms to myself. One will be a computer lab, another will be for me to have fun in with a high quality resolution big screen TV and all my video games. The other room can be as messy as I want it to be!

I have not seen my mom in the 6 months since I've been here. She's been told she has to have a steady address. She's had to work hard to get a Section 8 certificate. Now she has to use it. I miss her, but life's going to happen the way it's going to happen. You either accept it or you get mad over it. I'm not mad.

My life, so far, has taken some twists and turns, but so what? You always, somewhere in your mind, know the right choice. I think it's just natural to know what the right choice is. Life will always go forward and there'll always be a good way or a bad way. You just have to make the right choice.

Tyra

ALTHOUGH I WAS only five-years-old, I re-member everything as if it happened yesterday. In December 1985, my mother married her longtime boyfriend. After their marriage, things were pretty normal, but only for a short time. I remember going to the beach or the park and celebrating holidays.

However, there were moments when I would wake up to loud noises and screams and the sound of my mother crying because he was beating on her. I'll never forget one night when I woke up to them fighting. I was very scared and began to cry.

My room was across from theirs, and I was able to see a little bit of what was going on. When he heard me crying, he came into the room and looked at me and told me to shut up. I was very afraid of him, so I placed my blanket over my mouth until he left my room. The next thing I knew, the fight went from the bedroom to the dining room, right outside of my room. There was a bicycle chain on a chair and this man began to use it as he beat my mother. She managed to get away and ran outside for help. I waited a little bit before I ran to the kitchen and called my sister's house for help. As I ran back to my room, I could see drippings of my mother's blood all over the floor.

It wasn't long after that night that they had another fight. This time he didn't come back. From that day on there were many people in and out of my house. My mother stopped being a mother and turned to drug use. I no longer went to school on a regular basis. I wasn't fed sometimes. I can remember days where I'd be very hungry, but I wasn't fed because my mother was in such a deep sleep from her heavy drug use that she wouldn't wake up to fix me anything, despite my loud cries and shaking her. I either went without, or if I were lucky enough, someone who felt sorry for me would give me food.

I remember once I was so dirty and hadn't had a bath in such a long time that the bottoms of my feet were, literally, the color black. Despite my situation, it wasn't always bad. A girlfriend of one of the drug dealers looked out for me. She used to play games with me, take me for ice cream and make me Rice Krispie treats. Whenever she was around, my face lit up with joy. I was crazy about her. Sometimes I think if she had not been there for me, I would not have been able to make it some days.

My uncle was also a big help, whenever he was around. He always cooked me food and cleaned my clothes and room. They were the only two people in the house who made sure I was okay.

On my seventh birthday, my mother's husband came and took me out for lunch. When I returned, one of the drug dealers had bought me a birthday cake. My mother was in a deep sleep and wouldn't wake up to celebrate my birthday with me. Later that night, my sister took me out. When I came back, I tried to wake up my mother again, but she was in too deep of a sleep. She never woke up to see me on my birthday.

A few months later, a woman came to my house and had a meeting with my sister and my mother. I remember her words exactly. She said, "If you do not make any changes, we will remove Tyra from the home." My mother was so high I don't even think she knew what was going on.

In March of 1988, as I was walking toward the school bus, someone grabbed my shoulder. To my surprise, it was my sister. During the time of my mother's drug abuse she had come to get me every now and then, but she never came to my school. I immediately felt that something was wrong. She invited me to stay with her for a little while. I was seven and was thinking it was only for a few hours. When it got dark outside, I got suspicious that something was wrong. I said, in a broken voice, "I thought you said a little while." That turned out to be a few days, then a few weeks, months and, all together, eight years.

During four of those eight years I lived with my sister, her daughter and her husband, who didn't want me there. He used to argue with my sister because she wouldn't send me somewhere else. I'll never forget how he used to treat me so bad at times. I'll never forget how he once grabbed me by the wrists and placed my arms behind my back and hit me with a belt until I cried. Maybe if he had not laughed as he was doing it, I wouldn't have known that he enjoyed it.

In September 1992, my sister separated from her husband. He left us with nothing. My sister now had her seven-month-old son. For the first few months, we stayed with a friend until my sister got her own apartment. She was now going through a divorce with no job, no money, no family support and three children (including myself) to take care of. Times were very hard for all of us. Our new home was a tiny apartment with two bedrooms, a bathroom and a living room with a small space for a stove and a refrigerator. My sister's husband had taken the car, the house and the money.

Our own family knew we were going through hard times. My uncle was the only person to do anything. I'll never forget when he took us to the store and bought clothes for us and made sure we had food.

When my sister's new friend came around, her whole personality changed. Yet, when we moved in with him, my nightmare began. I was 13 by this time. I felt he was a control freak. We lived in his house and nothing was mine. We depended on him for everything. At one point, we were hungry and asked him for food. He said that he wasn't hungry. That was that.

When he felt that he was losing control, he would take things away from my sister, as well as us. More than once, he made us leave the house and took back everything he had given us. I would try to tell my sister how I felt about him doing things like that, but she wouldn't listen to me. My sister would tell him if I complained. Then he wouldn't speak to me. Once he didn't like how I had gotten my hair cut. He wouldn't talk to me then, either. I felt so trapped. I didn't see a future for myself.

I bought a journal. I wrote in it every day. The more I wrote, the more I noticed that I wasn't happy.

I realized that I was sad and depressed. I had never really been friendly with my social worker, but we started talking on the phone. Her name is Carla. On the phone I could express myself without my sister being around and getting mad at me. I could talk about how I was really feeling. I would look forward to coming home from school just so I could call Carla.

At one point my sister's boyfriend took us to Disneyland. He and my sister got into a fight, and he was going to leave us there without food or any way home. My uncle sent money and we were able to fly back home.

On June 26, 1996, after another fight, he began to pack up all of his things again. He took our furniture, TV's, food . . . you name it, he took it. My family knew. This man's nephews came and started taking apart our beds. I didn't know what was going to happen. I talked to my sister. She said, "If it weren't for you, I would have taken my kids and left." It was a stab in the heart.

I was tired of not knowing where I'd live, how I'd eat and especially tired of other people making bad decisions for themselves and ruining my life. I called Carla and said, "Can you please come and get me?"

When Carla picked me up, I was so upset. She talked to me about my options. I couldn't think straight. I didn't know what I wanted. I was scared. I decided to go to foster care. I needed a break. But I didn't know how long I'd be there. I stopped eating because I felt so stressed.

Between that day in June until February 24, 1997, I moved to eight foster homes and three residential programs. Those eight months were very challenging for me, but I can honestly say to this day that I have absolutely no regrets about leaving my sister's house.

February 27, 1997 I ended up at a new foster home. I didn't want to get out of the car. I was so tired of moving around. Finally, I went in. My foster mother was very nice. She helped me unpack. There was something really different about her.

She really cared about me. She talked to me and made sure I got what I needed. If I was sick, she would buy me medicine. She even talked to my therapist, so she could better help me. She was a real mother figure. She always included me in her family. I had never seen a family who had all been to high school and college, who went to work. Most of all, I had never seen a family who loved each other like they did.

After two months I even started calling my foster mother "Mom." I finally began to smile. I began to eat and to look forward to life. She helped me realize that a relationship is a mutual thing. You give and take. I did want to go back home. I used to call and remind my family of visits. They would cancel them anyway. Once my mother said to me, "I don't know if I can come visit you today because I'm supposed to go to a BBQ." My foster mother helped me understand that if they wanted to come, they would. I never had thought about that before. It was always me making the effort. It took nights of crying and emotional pain before I realized they were not going to be anything more than they already were. I honestly believe they don't know any better.

I'm very grateful to my sister for taking me in. I'm upset about some of her decisions, but I forgive her. She was just a child, herself, when she took me in and I feel she did a good job. I left, not because I hated her, but because I knew that if I wanted to have any type of change in my life and actually have a chance at succeeding, I had to leave altogether.

That phone call to Carla was one of the best decisions I ever could have made for myself. I have become a stronger person emotionally, physically and mentally, all because of that phone call.

My only regret is not calling sooner, so that I could have experienced more of the joy and love I've had with a wonderful foster family for the past four years now. I have since graduated high school with honors and I'm currently a freshman at college on nine scholarships.

On holidays, I return to the same home I went to in February 1997, where I have a family whom I love very much. Without their love in return, I don't know where I'd be. For those of you who have dreamed of something but were told it would never happen, I dedicate this story to you. I'm just one of millions who were told the same thing. Please don't ever let anybody tell you that you cannot achieve your dreams.

Tina

MY NAME IS Tina. I'm seventeen-years-old and I've been in foster care for three years. I grew up with my parents, sister and brother. I don't remember much. It was pretty normal, but some psychologist told me you block stuff out when you don't want to remember. I remember just a few little things.

When I was twelve, I started doing drugs. My dad was always at work. My mom was always sleeping. She always seemed depressed. When I'd ask her about it, she'd say it was none of my business. I said, "You're my mom. It is my business."

I stopped staying at home. I stayed with my best friend. Her mom used to treat me like a mom should. She would even make me my own vegetarian meals. She treated me like family. It felt better. I always liked being at someone else's house better than being at my own. My father would never be home. Everyone else I knew had relationships with their parents. I felt like the only one that didn't. It made me feel angry. Eventually, I got sad, too. Then I started be-coming a troublemaker, doing pot, drinking.

The more I was away, the worse it got with my parents. The worse it got with my parents, the more drugs I did. I started drinking every day. Everything seemed like it didn't matter. I would forget about my family problems and other problems when I was drunk and high. I stopped going to classes. Eventu-ally, I stopped going to school at all. (That was my freshman year, when I was fourteen). I slept all day and would stay up at night. My parents took me to the hospital. I spent time in a mental hospital for a week. They started giving me medication for depres-sion. I went home.

Then my social worker put me in a residential home for 30 days. I really didn't mind. I mean, at first I was wicked mad because it wasn't my choice, but then I started making friends with the people there. They wanted to give me people to talk with, to make sure I didn't do drugs.

I went back home. Every time I was taken back to my house, I'd be happy and say, "I'm going to change." But when I got back, I was just too angry at my parents. No one could ever really figure out why. I couldn't stand it. The only time I'd see my Dad was for five minutes before I left for school and that was it. He worked all day and all night.

My mom was there. When she talked to me, I'd just get mad at her. We'd go through cycles when she'd make me angry. Then, I'd do something to make her mad.

I've probably seen my parents hug once. I've never seen them kiss or hold hands. They were distant from each other and distant from me.

I hated myself. I felt no one else liked me, so

why should I like myself? My dad says my sister and I were close when we were little. When we were teenagers, we went our own ways.

My family never talked about stuff. If my parents found drugs in my room, they'd take them and not say anything about it. It confused me. They let me keep doing it. It seemed if they didn't say anything, it was okay to keep doing it. But if they had said anything, I know I would have done it anyway.

It seemed everything was going so fast, it was hard to figure things out. I was smoking weed, drinking, and by the time I was 15, I was doing 'shrooms, coke, acid, e, speed . . . I never did heroin. It just wasn't around.

Everyday was just about getting high or drunk. I wasn't interested in anything else. It seemed that if I didn't get messed up or drunk, that everything would fall apart. It actually felt like the drugs were holding me together. I was just getting rid of one problem by adding 20 more to my life. That one problem came back, always.

One day I was going to go out. My mom said no. I just left. I came home around 12:30 a.m. My mom was really mad and thinking about calling the cops. I didn't care, 'cause I was really messed up. My mom was mad for the next two days. We started fighting. I was going to take off. My father wouldn't let me leave. I had some drugs in my room. My dad was trying to get to my lockbox of drugs. I took it and my backpack and was trying to run. My dad wouldn't let me go. So I went downstairs and grabbed a knife from the kitchen. I said, "Stay away from me."

I finally got out of my house. I was going to run away. I didn't care. By the time I got to the end of the driveway, the police were there. They arrested

me. I ended up at a detention center and then went
to court. It didn't seem like it was real. I went to a
lock up.

It really was like a break from my life. They had
good food. There were things to do, like movies and
art classes. I was there for a few weeks. If I'd been
there longer, I would have said, "Let me out of here."
But for the time I was there, it was just a time off
from my life.

Then I was brought to a foster home. I was sad at
first, and mad. I didn't know how long I'd be here.
Then I started getting to know everybody. There
were three other foster children here. It changes all
the time from between three to five other teen girls
who stay here.

I thought I'd keep scoring. But Mona, my foster
mother, she listens. She respects you. She's been
around kids so long, she acts like one. I'd still see my
own mom once a week, or so. After that, I'd do drugs.

After five to seven months, I decided I didn't
want to do them anymore. The first time someone
asked, it was hard. The second time was hard, too,
but after being off them a month, I was at a point
where I didn't want to smoke or drink.

I was sick of being mad and depressed. It would
make it worse with the drugs. For the first time, I
cared about getting caught. I didn't want to leave
this foster home. Mona was awesome. She was like
someone to talk to—in between someplace like a
program and my house. It was perfect. It was a fun
place to be. I knew if I got busted, I'd lose it.

I told my social worker and Mona afterwards.
Mona was mad that I used at all, but we talked about
it. I started going to school again, but I was getting

suspended for disruptions. I ended up studying for the GED, and I passed the exam!

I'd see my parents every now and then. I had a counselor. I could tell him anything. He was really cool. He was someone to be there for me and not throw things back in my face. It helped me understand myself better and why my parents sometimes did the things that they did.

I've started working at a bank and taking classes at a community college. I'm studying psychology, English, math and writing. It's hard. I'm surprised that I could do this, but I have.

I have a good friend who has helped, as well as Mona and my counselor. I think you have to be the one to realize you need the help. Otherwise your counselor, foster mother or friend won't have a chance to help you.

Getting off the drugs, I could see more clearly. I didn't want to be a user. I was ready to grow up.

Justin

WHEN I WAS little, I lived in East Boston. There were a lot of people and kids right on top of each other, with all the apartments. I lived with my mom and my sister. Life was basically about hanging out at the Boy's Club, playing with the other kids. We were kind of poor, but I was happy. Most of the time I had what I needed. I knew things weren't 100% normal though.

My mom has a lot of ups and downs with drug and alcohol abuse. When I was really young, we lived with a foster family for a few months because of that. My mom was doing well for awhile. Then, when I was six or seven, she went to rehab or jail. I can't remember which because she spent time in both.

I lived with one of her friends. I had to stay back in first grade because my paperwork got lost and they thought I was out of school. Then we were back with my mom and things were going well again. We moved a few times, but mostly within a few blocks.

My mom went out every now and then, but wasn't

drinking a lot. Then she got bad again, when I was about twelve. It was really rough. She wasn't coming home all the time. I remember working and trying to keep things cool at home and stuff. I was trying to hold down things, get my sister's school clothes and supplies and make sure she still went to school.

I was working a lot at a liquor store. I sorted out bottles and cleaned up for some extra money. They used to pay me in cash, subs and beer. That got me into a drinking problem by the time I was going into seventh grade. I stopped going to school because my mom really wasn't pushing me to go. When I'd go, I'd go drunk. Some people started noticing what was going on. I don't know who called DSS, but they got involved.

We moved into my grandparent's house in Lynn. They were strict. There were different rules in a different atmosphere. Lynn was a tough environment. I started hanging out with an all right crowd, though, and stopped drinking and smoking cigarettes. We lived there for about a year.

Then I moved in with some of my mom's old friends, who had moved to the suburbs. My mother was back in jail again. I felt like she was safe in jail, until I found out you could get drugs there, too. I didn't know how long it would be until I saw her again.

I started eighth grade in Ipswich. I was a city kid, dressing and talking very differently. I started hanging out with kids who were more like me. I didn't like where I was staying, even though these folks were treating us really well. I was just going through a lot of stuff, so I was really acting up.

I got involved with a youth group at a Baptist Church. That really helped. They met once a week on Sundays and then I'd go to a Tuesday group. I ended up doing a lot of peer leadership groups. I felt good. It gave me something to feel good about.

When I was a junior in high school, I became a youth leader and started working with the younger kids. My friends and I had started a band the year before. I'm 20 now, and we're still together. We do a lot of funky stuff . . . a lot of jazz and blues. I had a part time job, too, at a restaurant. It was all cool, but a little too much.

I had a lot on my plate and wasn't able to give a hundred per cent to anything. I felt like I just had to keep busy. I needed to keep my mind off things. I didn't keep school as my number one priority either. It felt a little overwhelming. I'm still learning about that.

All the way through my life though, from when I was little, I had a lot of people stepping in and helping me out.

In East Boston, an afterschool activities director took a liking to me and got me involved in peer leadership in the middle school there. In Lynn, another person took me under his wing. I had a lot of counselors and teachers pushing me and telling me I was meant to do something really good. I listened to that. I figured if a lot of people were saying the same thing, I must be doing something right.

Then, my youth group leaders and foster mothers gave me a lot of confidence. One of my foster mothers let me play her bass. I play the bass today.

As I got near high school graduation, I got scared about college. My DSS Outreach worker, Erin, got me a scholarship and pushed me to go to school. I waited until the last minute, but I went to North Shore Community College, close to where I lived. I kept my girlfriend, job and band.

This summer I'm studying at Berklee College of Music. I'll take a music program at The University of Massachusetts this fall. Then I want to finish at Berklee, studying production and engineering. I am learning a lot.

My mom is living with my grandparents now, and doing well. She's going to take me out for my 21st birthday. All the things that have mattered have stayed the same. I've had the same girlfriend for three to four years now. My band is still together. We have a manager. My friends have stuck with me. I have a good relationship with my foster parents. Hopefully, I'll be moving out on my own soon. I'll have fun being an adult!

Honestly, all the bad stuff was a test. I had to keep pushing through it. If I gave up, then, I'd fail the test. You've got to work with what you've got. It's as if life is like a Marathon. You can be running along and then you get tripped up. You can stay down and look as the people pass you or you can get on your feet and trust in inspiration to get back in the lead again. I had to get there.

Patricia (Patty)

HELLO. MY NAME is Patricia. However, most people call me Patty. This is my story.

I grew up in Boston. During my childhood I lived in a housing unit with my two older sisters, my mom, and sometimes my father. My mother is bipolar and schizophrenic. Dad wasn't always around because he was in and out of jail, mainly for hitting my mom, but once he was in for stabbing a cop. He didn't get out for a while after that. I think this was why he wasn't there for my birth. When he was home, he was just talking to himself. I don't have too many memories of Daddy dearest. Most of my memories are of being severely abused, both emotionally and physically all throughout childhood. I remember being very poor. I was never the kid with the new bike or clothing. Everything I owned was second hand. School lunch was store-brand peanut butter over store-brand white bread and milk in a thermos. On holidays, our church supplied dinner, and a rich family sponsored our gifts on Christmas.

My mother did the best she could. I truly believe this. We may not have been the richest kids, but we got lots of love. No matter what my mother did to us, she still always loved us. My sister who is a year and a half apart from me became my best friend throughout childhood. We looked out for each other. We never really fought. Today we are close. I think we used each other to survive. As for our older sister, she never bothered with us. That lack of bonding has left my close sister and me on bad terms with her.

I also have two older brothers. One is twenty-eight and the other was 25 when he died. My parents lost custody of my brothers when they were very young. They grew up in foster homes far from my family and me. Visiting was set up for one hour a month. I never had enough time with them when I was little. When I grew up, I built a relationship with the oldest brother. My other brother was murdered in September '99. I never built a bond with him. Losing my brother made me feel so alone. I blamed myself for not spending enough time with him and I still do. Knowing the pain he endured and that I'll never get him back plays itself over and over again in my mind. I feel like I've lost a part of myself forever.

My mother and I started having a lot of problems when I was fifteen. I'll admit some of it was my fault. However, my mother was mainly to blame. She gave me no freedom. I wasn't allowed to see my friends and spent a lot of time in my room. I got very frustrated and started letting my built up frustration out on my mom. She called me disobedient. Really, I was a great kid who just needed a little space. I started dating my fiancé at the time. This really didn't go over too swell with my mom. She got a restraining order on him under false pretenses. Then she took me to the courthouse one lovely morning. By the end of the day I was signed over to DSS under a CHINS, a court order for a Child In Need of Services. I was very scared and didn't know what to expect. Once in care, I missed my mother. My foster family was all right, but they weren't my own. I saw a lot less of my close sister. Over time, I was switched to two more homes, the second of which I remained in until I was 18. During this time my sister and I grew apart. We've managed to recover a lot of our closeness, but not everything can remain as it used to.

My long-term foster family turned out to be great. It took a little while and some change on my part for things to really work. We just had to get used to each other. I didn't get along with them in the beginning and they didn't seem to like me very much. The feeling was mutual. They told me a lot of things that I didn't want to hear. After a little while I started getting closer to them and listening to their advice. They helped me to grow. I went in a naïve teenager and came out a smart and sensible young woman. Time brings change and I grew to love them and accept them. In the end, leaving them to move on felt like it had when I first left home.

My experiences in my foster home helped me to come to reality and start making some changes for my future. I got a lot of support from DSS. I made plans for graduating high school and moving on to college. I didn't have to do it alone. My foster mother helped me with my PAYA (preparation for independent living) books so that I had an understanding of life on my own. My sister and real mom were always there for moral support. My foster brother and sister always gave me good advice. My social worker never gave up faith in me or let me go astray. She always helped me when I needed it. DSS set me up in my own apartment. They help me with the rent. I have a wonderful independent living worker who went through the process of helping me in finding furniture for my apartment, budget planning, and applying for colleges, none of which could have been fun for her. She did it because she really cares. I had lots of friends and caring adults on my side. I found that if I worked with people and put in my fair share, I was never rejected. I had faith in myself and trust of others who weren't always there.

I'm still 18 and will be starting college in the fall and I am engaged to be married after I've finished school. I maintain a part time job at a restaurant. My money goes in the bank for part of my rent and for the future, when I'm no longer in care. I'm very responsible now. I feel great about myself.

My advice to children and teens in foster care would be to hang in there. It only gets better as long as you try. I understand in the beginning there are so many questions and concerns. You may not like being in care. I was the same way. I was the one who never thought I'd be doing what I'm doing today. I never thought I'd say this, but please trust me when I say that DSS can only help you. That's what they do. That's why they had me tell you my story. They care and don't want you to be scared. It's lonely in the beginning but you have to give it a chance. Don't end up in trouble and in programs. It's only a waste of time. It won't get you back home. It'll end up keeping you away longer. I wasn't always the best kid, but I had some smarts. They paid off.

Take advantage of all the resources DSS has to offer you. You have an advantage over most kids. Don't let it go to waste. Do the best with what you're dealt. Good luck!

Neddy

MY EARLIEST MEMORY is of getting up in the morning and fixing breakfast for my younger sister, Angie, and myself. My birth mother was an addict, and although she never mistreated us, she wasn't available to care for us. I was no more than four or five-years-old at the time. By the time I was six, I had a baby brother to care for, as well. I rarely made it to school. I don't recall resenting this. It was the only life I knew, and I was perfectly content.

My mother was arrested and I went to live with a family friend. It is hard to remember the next few months. I know there was a lot of bouncing around from friends to relatives to a couple of foster homes before my sister and I finally landed together in the same home. My brother went elsewhere and we rarely saw him. Around this time, I found out that my birth mother was pregnant again. That was the first time I remember getting really angry with her. Until then, I was always quick to make excuses for her. I loved my mom very much, in spite of everything she could not do for us, but this time there was no excuse for her behavior.

When I think about the things that helped during this really hard time, I would have to point to several things. The most important was being able to live in a foster home with my sister. The second was having a consistent social worker who really listened to me. I also had a therapist. John was great. Having a place to unload all of my grief and anger really helped. Then there was school. I wasn't a great student but I always tried hard and my teachers seemed to like me. Sports and music were the places I shined.

The hardest part was being separated from my baby brother. For all intents and purposes, I had been his mother all of his seven months of life. I know my birth mother had lost several children to state custody before I was born, but they weren't real to me. He was, and I worried about him all the time.

I actually liked my first long-term home but there was a major problem. They liked me, too! Why not? I was quiet, compliant, and helpful. But they didn't like my sister. Angie was very strong willed and very angry about being away from our mother. It was terrible to watch her constantly being punished. Sometimes I thought about acting up just so she wouldn't feel so alone.

Things came to a head the summer I was seven. My foster family was going on vacation. They wanted to take me, on a pre-adoptive trial, but wouldn't take Angie. They were definitely not interested in adopting her. Once again, I was torn. I had never been on vacation before, but I hated leaving my sister behind, especially since I had no idea where she would be going. Suddenly, as is often the case when you are a foster child, I heard that Angie was moving to a new home. I was happy for her. She was going to live with her pre-school teacher and I knew she would be a lot happier being the only little girl, but I was devastated.

I went on vacation and Angie moved the same week. We visited a lot, but it wasn't the same. Apparently, there was a lot of discussion about what to do with us. We couldn't go home. My birth mother was not able to stay clean. Some social workers were really committed to Angie and me being placed together. Others were just as committed to children being placed in racially appropriate homes. I don't recall anyone asking my opinion. I just remember, once again, packing up to go live with strangers. This time, I was the outsider, going to live in my sister's foster home.

I don't remember when I realized that this time was different. For one thing, this wasn't a real foster home. We were the only foster children. The three older boys in this house didn't seem to hate us. From the beginning, they treated us like sisters. They were so wonderful throughout the whole transition and the rest of my growing up days. When other boys would pick on me, my brothers were the ones I could run to and tell, and immediately defense would be on my side. I can't recall a time when any of my three brothers and I actually got into a serious fight. Yeah, sure, there have been the occasional arguments over different opinions, but that's all. That is why, to this day, we are all so very close.

For several months, we were all on our best behavior. But after a bit, the honeymoon was over. I still had school, sports, and music to center me, but I fought some real control battles with my new mother. I never had a mother before, and as I reached ten, I discovered I didn't really want one now. Things with my new father, however, were easier.

The year I turned 11 was one of the changes. My social worker, Nancy, told me that we would be getting a new worker because the plan now was for us to be adopted by our foster family. Although I was very delighted to have some sort of closure to this long journey in my life, I was also very confused and still didn't understand why my mother didn't want my sister and me. I guess that was something that I have overcome in these past years.

In spite of all these harsh feelings and memories, I have a wonderful life now. I am now a senior in high school and I've been on the varsity soccer and softball team for four years. I was just the captain of the soccer team this past fall, and I'm going to be the captain of the softball team this spring. I have been in the school choir for four years as well. I am very active in many school-run productions as well as extra-curricular activities, such as being an official for young kids soccer leagues. I was also the coordinator of the elementary school tutor program and was also a tutor for two years.

As you can see, I thoroughly enjoy helping people. So as I enter my next school year in the fall, I plan to attend college and pursue a career in Criminal Justice and become a juvenile probation officer to help kids stay out of trouble. . .to help them realize there is an alternative life for them besides what is being offered and to make advantage of every available opportunity life has to offer.

Angie

I HAVE ALWAYS considered myself lucky. Looking back on my childhood, I realize that children who live in the same conditions I did and have had the same lifestyle I did don't always make it. I now understand that I was an exception. I made it.

My sister and I lived with our mother and little brother in a tiny apartment in Amherst, MA. It wasn't considered top notch, but that's all my mother could afford. To us it was a "stomping ground," a place we would call home, a place that held some of our most terrifying memories.

There are times I remember my older sister putting on the "parent suit", many times where she would change a diaper or cook our meals. Neddy has always been the one that I counted on; she was the glue that held our family together. I can still see her hovering over the stove on a chair, five years old, and cooking scrambled eggs. Our mother was nowhere to be found, but the thought that she was looking for drugs was never far from my mind. Something happened and Neddy burned herself, but no one would have known. She showed no flicker of pain. In a way, she couldn't. That would be considered letting me and my brother down.

One night, my mother and one of her boyfriends had gotten into an argument and started screaming and hitting each other. It was so terrifying when my mother pulled out a kitchen knife and started threatening him. Neddy held me so close and pulled me behind the couch as we cried. We were both shaking in each other's arms as the fighting progressed. It went on for hours. Neddy felt my pain. She understood much more than I did. She understood fights like these happened over drugs and money and that this wasn't how a family was supposed to work. Neddy understood that.

I've always had this connection with my mother that, no matter what she did, I would erase it from my mind and she would be a saint again. We were always dragged around with her on her escapades, whether it was running from a taxi driver that she didn't pay, or being caught by the police for stealing grocery carts full of food. It wouldn't be her fault that she didn't think twice about bringing us along for a car ride. She would shoot up heroin as we watched her from the front seat. How could she help having a seizure from overdosing in front of us?

Those things didn't seem to be her fault. She couldn't help them. Even the fact that we were put into foster care . . . that was my fault. I was the bad kid that she didn't want.

The day the social worker took us away was the start of an incredible journey into the world of foster parents, lawyers and, eventually, adoption. As you can imagine, the first step wasn't paradise . . . being torn from my mother, my memories and the only life that I knew. I was miserable from the second I stepped into that first home, but at least all of us were together.

A few days later, we were taken away again, to more unknown territory, except that this time we didn't get to take our brother. Slowly, we were losing everything that had meaning to us.

All my life, my sister had been the one that people preferred more. I was always the one they had a harder time connecting to. I was the difficult child, harder to get along with. I felt like I was an embarrassment. I would go to pre-school and act up, just to get it out of my system. There was one teacher, Mrs. Harrison, who seemed to understand.

She minded it, when I fought with the other kids and wouldn't share the Play-Doh, but she understood that there was more to me. Mrs. Harrison was the one that I told mostly everything to. I was surprised that she listened to me, and she believed me. She really seemed to care. She opened up a whole new world of opportunities for me.

Mrs. Harrison decided to become a foster parent. She really wanted to take care of me, to treat me the way all five-year olds should be treated. This was like a dream come true.

I was small for my age, barely reaching forty pounds, with long, scraggly, black hair and enormous almond eyes. My legs were swinging nervously beneath me while I waited to be picked up. My sister was going to be left behind this time. The car pulled up. I picked up my little brown paper bag with my belongings and went to greet my new foster mother. By this time, I was really used to the idea of moving and the thought that no one really wanted me was well tattooed on my mind. I knew this was different. I knew Mrs. Harrison on a totally different level from any other adult. Everything felt different about her. It all felt right.

A whole new life began the minute I buckled myself in to that front seat. I felt a new feeling, that things would be okay.

Yet, I also remember that at first I didn't have any trust. I thought, "What's the point of getting attached if I'm just going to leave in a couple of days?" I acted up so Mom would get sick of me, and I'd get it over with. My mom wouldn't give up on me and I realized this was for real. I kept telling my foster mother, who I now called Kathryn, all about my past. The only key to that was my sister. So the Harrisons made a huge decision to take in Neddy, as well. Kathryn wanted us to be together and a few months later, Neddy came to live with us. Everything was still a dream. In a couple of years Neddy and I would be adopted by the Harrisons and finally have a family of our own.

Meantime, I frequently thought about my biological mother and wondered whether she cared or remembered. She would send letters. Neddy and I cried when we read what she was going through. Her months in jail and an arm length's worth of promises . . . all these things made living in paradise so much harder.

Every night I screamed at the top of my lungs before it was time to go to bed. I would intentionally wet the bed and I always acted up. Right from the start, I had thought it was my fault . . . that my mother didn't want me. This way, by acting up, I would get sent back to her.

But Kathryn saw past all that. She was willing to

give me the time I needed to cool off. Every night, before I went to bed, she read to me until I was asleep. In the morning, she made secret visits to see if I was dry, so that I wouldn't feel embarrassed in front of the others. Everything she did made being away from my mother easier to understand.

Just as it seemed we were finally getting settled and comfortable, my sister and I got notice that my mother had AIDS and, someday, we would never see her again. This killed me. I can't remember how long it took to stop crying. I would look at a picture of her for hours, with tears streaming down my face. I wanted to be with her more than anything. But a part of me knew my fantasy of living with her was over.

Everytime we set up a visitation, she wouldn't show and we would wait for an hour. Yet, all I wished for was to be with her. I knew this would hurt Kathryn, to know that with all that she gave us, it would be hard to part with our mother. But she was there for us, to comfort us and always let us talk to her about what we were going through.

I admit that during this time, I acted up more than anything. I was rude and disrespectful. I would tell Kathryn she wasn't going to tell me what to do, that she wasn't my "real" mom. I fought with my brothers. School wasn't much different. I always acted up and wrote nasty words on pieces of paper and threw them all around my classroom. I was miserable. I thought, "Maybe this will do the trick and they'll send me back to my mom."

At the same time, I felt my mother should fight harder for us. I felt it was my fault. When she gave us up, it was hard to understand why she didn't fight harder.

Kathy wouldn't give up. She brought me to therapy. My therapist became my best friend. She allowed me to express myself in her office. Erica just understood. She gave me these dolls. I'd act out and role-play. It helped to talk about it. She was the second adult I trusted. Everything stayed between us. I had someone to talk to about my life who wouldn't share it. It really helped. Every other aspect of my life was so public. Everyone, all the social workers knew my story. But Erica could understand how I felt. I knew I wouldn't get in trouble for my feelings.

It changed my perspective on grown-ups. I realized if I could trust her, then I could trust others. I talked to my mom about my biological mother. I was able to open up more in my family. There were no secrets.

I just know that after we talked about getting adopted, I felt so good that I was going to have a family that loved me.

My brother played clarinet. He taught me when I was in third grade. I also started playing soccer. I wouldn't have had that anywhere else. It made me feel like my mom really loved me because she wanted me to be involved in all this. It gave me confidence that I could actually go through with this, and be strong, and actually have a life. I'm a junior in high school now and I still play soccer and my clarinet.

We went to church. I didn't understand it. But that's where I made friends who are still my friends to this day. This girl took to me and we'd play. She actually wanted to be my friend. It was great to have a friend my own age, not a teacher or therapist. I hadn't gotten along with peers before that. My friends have stuck by me all the way.

Now, I am active in drama, band and my church.

I also participate in parent training classes for foster parents. I feel like I know both sides of the fence, and it has made me stronger. This foster care journey has taught me so much. I have shared the lives of over 60 other children who have come into our home for foster care. They suffered like I did. My mom gives them exactly what it takes to lessen the grieving process.

As I look at the big things for me, I see that there were points in time where I'd give up. I'd feel there was no hope. I felt no one had feelings for me, just my sister. These are stages you go through. You'll get over it. When people come into your life who are actually willing to be there for you, you have to realize who they are. I had to figure out who was there for me and who was just walking through my life.

To this day, my mom and I have a great relationship. I work hard to keep it that way because she means so much to me. My sister and I look back and say "Wow, we had to go through so much just to get here." It's hard to realize it when you've had so many false hopes. It can be hard to distinguish, but there are people who are going to fight hard for you and it's just a great feeling when you finally realize that.

Alicia

W̲HEN I WAS young, I lived with my mother. I kind of bounced around. We would stay with whoever her current boyfriend was. We lived with my aunt for a while. Life was very confusing. I never really knew what was going on. My mother would be out all night with whomever, doing whatever. She would be drunk and passed out.

My family says I'd mimic her cocaine use: putting a straw up my nose or using dollar bills. I didn't really know exactly what it was. I thought it was a natural thing. I was three.

My brother used to ask me what she was doing when she was snorting or smoking cocaine. I'd say, I didn't know. She'd do it at the kitchen table when we were sitting there.

My mother had four children. My parents had three children together. My mother was only sixteen when she had me. When one of my sisters was born, a year after I was, my mother gave her to my father's sister. My aunt has raised her.

It was me, my brother, my other sister and a cousin. I was like the mom. It was hard. I didn't really know what I was doing. I made sure we'd all eat. I'd try to make French toast, but it never came out. I don't think I cooked it long enough. We'd microwave dinners.

My dad was in jail most of the time. He dropped off the face of the earth when I was about nine. When I did see him, it was never scheduled. He was never in my life fully, even when I was a baby.

My mother always depended on different guys, and they always paid for everything. We really never knew where she was. I used to get upset, calling her boyfriends' houses looking for her. She'd get mad. Once she spanked me for it.

I remember when she got married. I didn't want that because they used drugs together and I didn't like that. Sometimes it was scary. When the whole DSS thing started, I didn't know why we were being taken away. I was seven.

My mother brought us to a foster home. She said, "You're going to stay here for a little while, while I go get better." That never happened.

A little while ended up being almost 12 years.

Her ex-husband's mother and father became our foster parents. Life in foster care was different. We weren't used to rules, but we got used to it. Things were great. We went to school and made friends. We had lots of opportunities.

We were able to do typical childhood things, like go to Disney World. My brother and I are both still wards of the state. There was never a legal guardianship. My foster mother feels like my mother, though. She raised us.

Yet, we always hoped that we'd get back with

our mother. I never realized she wasn't going to be better until my high school graduation day. A couple of weeks before, she said, "I'll be at your graduation, even if I have to come in a wheelchair." She really wanted to be there. I did want her to be there, too. She'd been clean for a while, so I was hoping she'd be on the right track.

When I looked for her at the ceremony, I didn't see her. I shrugged it off. I wasn't going to let it get to me. It was my day.

She did show up at my graduation party, two hours after it started. She showed up with a woman who was her "sponsor". They were both really high and dressed like tramps.

They were only there for a short time. Her friend asked for the bathroom. Then she asked for it again a few minutes later.

When she came out, she had her jacket and told my mom they had to leave.

Meantime, my sister had gone into the bedroom. She couldn't find her backpack. I went into my room. I was putting some more graduation money into a treasure chest that I had. It was gone. That money was for a computer for me to take to college. We didn't have a good time after that.

I felt more angry than anything. I couldn't believe it. I thought we were her stopping point. I didn't think she'd ever do anything to hurt me like that.

One of my social workers had given me a gold bracelet. That had been in the box, too. After that, my foster mother called the police. I was just in a daze, in shock.

My sister and other family went looking for my mother. They found her in a bar with her "sponsor" and a boyfriend. The police couldn't find anything but a crack pipe on the "sponsor". I was leaving for Florida the following Friday. That Wednesday she got arrested for breaking and entering.

I felt relieved that she was off the street. I was sick and stressed and thought, "Good, she deserves it!" I was very mad.

I talked to my social worker. She had said at my graduation that a successful life like mine makes her job worth it. She was so proud. It turns outs that she had called the DSS Public Affairs office. A week or two after I got back, one of my other social workers called and said, "Can I stop by? We pulled some strings in Boston. Lewis Howe is here and we're bringing a donated computer."

So they showed up at my house with cards and gifts and the computer. I was very touched that they actually did that for me. The computer was an older one that had been reconditioned. The hard drive crashed, though. My foster mother called the Public Affairs office again. Lewis called back and said, "Go to Staples and pick out another." They donated a brand new one to me!

The local paper published the story and people started sending me money, teddy bears and sweatshirts. It was something to see how people will do nice things for people. One woman has become my pen pal. She's in her seventies. She sends me cards all the time. I'm going to stop by her house soon to meet her.

It encourages me.

Growing up, I was kind of embarrassed and hurt when people said, "Why don't you live with your mother?" People judge people. Just because my mother uses drugs doesn't make me a bad person. I know what I don't want for my own children. I think this will help me become a good parent.

I watched my sister's stepmother take care of her mother when she was dying a couple of years ago. Something touched me about that. I want to take care of people. I'm in my freshman year at college now, studying nursing.

What kept me on track was looking at what my mother did and knowing I didn't want to be like that. My foster mother has given up so much for us. She raised her own kids. This was her time to retire, to be with her husband, and instead she took us in. It was amazing. I'm so glad somebody cared.

Seeing how many people actually do care about me is really something.

Anthony

I'M TWENTY-TWO YEARS old now. I grew up in Boston and came into foster care because of a difficult home life. DSS had already been involved with my older siblings. When I became a teenager, my mother had a hard time with my growing up. By the time I was fourteen, my mother had two much younger children. There were toddlers running around, as well as me at home. Their fathers weren't around. My father wasn't around. We lived in the projects, on welfare.

I got into Boston Latin High School, which is a very good school. It's hard to be admitted and the work is very challenging. The more I grew up, the more difficult things became with my mother. She would yell at me a lot and berate me. Boston Latin is a hard school and I had trouble staying on top of things. Yet, there was nothing at home to support me.

The harder school got, the worse it got at home. My mother would scream at me. She would abuse me a lot, verbally. She would insult my intelligence and that made me feel bad about myself. So, I wasn't focusing and ended up not responding well to anything around me. I started to get in trouble at school. I got suspended for fighting. Then, my mother would yell at me more. She wasn't able to help me through it. We ended up screaming at each other.

I tried to run away and she called the police. I spent the weekend in jail. After that, DSS came into the picture. The court decided that I should go into foster care. I bounced from group homes to shelters, for several months over the summer vacation between my freshman and sophomore year.

I started back at Boston Latin in a shelter. I didn't know anyone and I'd never really been away from my family. I wasn't allowed to leave, yet it was hard to deal with what was there. All the other kids seemed like seasoned veterans. They knew the system and how to work it. I felt really out of my element.

I couldn't adjust to any one place because I was always moving. School was even more challenging, but I managed to do okay. In the late fall, I finally got placed in a foster home. That was really good. I stayed with my foster mother until I was eighteen.

It was an awesome placement for me. The environment was very caring. My foster mother was really patient and understanding of the issues I had and the fact that I came with my own problems and quirks. I knew I wouldn't be yelled at the minute I stepped in the door.

Yet, I was angry at first about being in foster care. It was hard to live with a family I didn't know and had no experience with. What carried me through was the knowledge that I needed to do something with myself.

I refused to let the situation take control of my life. Something inside told me not to give up. I wanted to finish high school, go to college and do something with myself. During this time, I got a lot of support for my interests and the stability was just what I needed. I did really well at debate. My foster mother took me to a month–long debate forum up in Maine, and even took me around to look at colleges.

I did really well in school during my junior and senior year. In debate, I was state champion for the Lincoln Douglas Debates my senior year, and ended up placing third in New England as well.

When I was eighteen, I went to the University of Massachusetts (UMass-Boston). I got my own apartment. My Outreach workers helped me focus. They helped me as I learned how to manage my money, go to work and school and keep a balanced schedule. I'm graduating from college with a double major in philosophy and art. I haven't seen my birth mother in 8 years. I will at some point, but I'm just not ready.

I'm about to join DSS to become an Outreach worker, myself. It's my responsibility to give back, after what I've received. It's incumbent upon me to share my experiences with others. I think I can do a lot of good.

Euridece

FOR WHAT I have been through you have to believe in faith. I have fought all these injuries. I don't want to sound like a hero, but I have come so far.

I didn't have a mother who praised me, but if I know who I am, it's okay. I'm proud of myself. My standards are very high for myself, but that's okay. A couple of years ago I wouldn't have said this, but I like myself. I love myself. Being alive is great at this point.

I was born and raised in Cape Verde by my father and grandmother until I was nine. My father was wonderful! He used to tell stories. I loved being with him very much. My mother had moved to Boston. She came and took me to the United States with her. My father thought it would be better for me there. There is more opportunity in this country for education and for a good job. He was looking out for me. The outcome was not what we expected.

My mother was a stranger to me. She was always out working. I cooked and took care of myself. It was very lonely. I could barely speak the language. My mother was never there. It was really hard. My mother believed hitting was discipline. Things would come flying across the room at me. But when harsh things are being said to you, does a beating even matter? I was nine years old and I didn't know what hurt me more, her beatings or her words.

It was emotional chaos. Her words were so harsh. Who could I lean on? My mother said I was disgraceful and many other things as well. I used to think about having a mom who would protect me and keep me safe.

Once my mother hit me so hard that I had horrible bruising on my face. The school nurse asked me what happened and I tried to cover up. I made up a story about falling.

When I was ten, I got a dance scholarship at the Cambridge Project. It's an organization that goes into schools to teach kids. I loved it! Modern dance is a way of expressing yourself, how you feel, how you hear the music, and how you look at the world. It's always original. It's always your own work, your own experience. My teacher used to say, "Just dance!"

It was so therapeutic and healing. It made me free. I can fly, walk, run, and sing. I can be anything for that one moment. I was asked to be part of the Back Porch Dance Company. I danced with this interracial company of women for five years. They were like 15 mothers taking care of me!

My mother's best friend ended up taking me in. She lost her friendship with my mother, but she opened her heart to me and she never rejected me. I called her "Mom" and her husband, "Dad." Their four daughters are my sisters. She taught me how to live again. It wasn't always easy, but she supported me. I had been an honor student with perfect attendance, but that had never mattered to me. Now, my foster mother came to my school events and performances. It gave me hope regardless of the fact that my real mother wasn't there for me. This woman cared. That's when my life changed.

I took control of what life meant. My foster mother taught me how to love again, to feel love for the people I care about. That was hard at first. She also showed me that it is okay to feel anger, to just let it out.

My dance teacher and I became very close at this point. Bridget saw me through it all. She took me under her wing and taught me proper dance technique. She also helped me to see again who I was and where I was going with my life. She'd say, "With your smile, you can go anywhere." We are still close. We can talk about anything.

I lived for a while with a social worker. Maggie encouraged me to talk. "How do you feel?" she'd ask me. "What do you think about your mother?" She had energy for her kids and me and her friends. She was an inspiration.

I got an "Exceptional Scholarship" and was accepted to the State University of New York at Brockport. College was tough at first. I didn't feel prepared to go on. I still had a lot to learn about where I was going. My writing skills were not that good, and it was difficult, academically. Sharing a room was hard too. I also experienced racism, which was not easy.

My advisor asked the school to give me another chance. My second year was better. I felt like I was finally ready, that I could do it. I lived with four friends. We had private bathrooms, which helped. I took on some of the racial problems, too.

Finally, I can say I know where I'm going. I know what I want. I'm a grown woman. I'll graduate next spring with a BA degree, majoring in dance and with a minor in Spanish. I'm going to audition for different companies. I may work at Americorps, using my dance skills to help others. I love kids. I feel the childhood I never had when I'm around kids. I'd love to teach. I have something to give.

My mother and I have a great "geographical" relationship. That's what I call it. We get along great when we are out of each other's faces. She went through a crisis when I was young. Now, we get along really well whenever I come to Boston. I don't hold onto grudges. I don't know how I forgave her. I just have no intention of hating her for the rest of my life.

Don't feel bad for me. This has made me what I am. There are times when I wonder what I'd be like if I had had a normal life, but at this point, it's full. It will get fuller. I'm looking forward to it.

I have always believed God is watching over me and I truly know love can conquer everything.

Jennifer

I AM EIGHTEEN years old. When I was young, I thought I had everything a girl could possibly want. I had two wonderful parents, an older brother and all the love one could obtain. I was happy and I loved my family very much. We would take long trips to the Quabbin Reservoir, where I climbed towers. My brother and I would roll down the huge hills of dandelions. We would also have quiet nights at home, watching movies.

All that shifted when my parents divorced. My mom was clinically ill. Later, my brother was diagnosed with an illness, too, which explained why he sometimes abused me. My father was oblivious to this. I, regretfully, kept it a secret, thinking it was all my fault. I closed myself off from life and became depressed.

My father remarried. I had a new family to adapt to, yet I fell in love with my stepmother and stepbrothers quickly. Yet, for some reason, I was still not satisfied with my life.

I was in high school at this point. It was then, sophomore year, that I met Nick. He became my protector, my love, my life. We became so infatuated with each other that I closed myself off from my family and the tension grew between my parents and me.

I wanted to seek my individuality when they wanted me to sit in front of the television with the family. It was hard to deal with. Neither of us was entirely right.

So I began running away whenever my parents and I had a fight. I would go to Nick's house whenever this happened. Once, after not showing up for three days, my father put a CHINS (Child In Need of Services) petition on me. The police showed up at school the next day and took me out of class. It was one of the scariest things I've ever gone through.

They put me in a holding cell for five hours. That's when I went into foster care, and I was more happy than sad at the time. I just couldn't live with my parents, but I was scared about what place I'd be put into.

Luckily, a friend of mine, Tiffany, talked to her mother about me and they accepted me into their family. I became a sister, something I thought I would never be. It was hard to adapt to a new family's rules and lifestyle, but I was willing to do anything to turn my life around. My foster mother gave me confidence in myself and taught me things that, to this day, I still remember. Tiffany and I used to have pillow fights and exercise to Cindy Crawford videos every day.

Whenever I felt discouraged, I went to Tiffany or Charlotte, my foster mother. They always gave me the best advice, and it was memorable.

I became less dependent on my boyfriend and prepared myself for a new life: college. My Outreach worker, Bernadette, helped me find a college that was suitable for me.

Now, I am at the University of Massachusetts/ Boston, majoring in psychology. I have an apartment near Boston University, right in the city, and have a great roommate. I see my natural mother every now and then, and I try to visit my family whenever I can. Nick and I broke up. Yet, we've remained good friends ever since. My foster sister, Tiffany, also goes to school in Boston and we see each other every week.

DSS helps me financially with my rent and is always there for my questions and needs. I have a better life because of foster care.

My parents and I have a better relationship. At the same time, I've gained a new life. All it took was a little self-discipline and the help of DSS and the people around me. I consider myself a lucky young woman.

I just want to let all of you know that you can accomplish anything if you put your mind to it. And in relationships, don't let anybody make you something you're not. Be yourself and stand up for what is right. If you are a person like me, who had a rough childhood, all I can say is, everything is a learning experience.

Everything happens for a reason, and you can succeed no matter what anyone tells you. You are in charge of your own destiny. And there are tons of people out here willing to help you. I believe in you, just as I learned to believe in myself.

Gary Z.

BEFORE WE WERE split up, I lived with my four older sisters and two older brothers. We were all separated by about a year in age. How did I feel about my family? I loved 'em to pieces. The best experiences I can remember were the times we were all playing together.

We really had some fun times. On the other hand, the worst experience I remember is when my sisters dressed me up like a ballerina. I'm still mad at my sisters for the ballerina thing!

My father left my mother, who was twenty-six at the time. He did nothing to help my siblings and me. Then my mom became sick, and all seven of us were placed in foster care. We all went to separate homes. Our big family was shattered. I was confused and, I think, I felt pretty mad. Getting ripped away from my parents was bad enough . . . but from my siblings, who were my best friends . . . that was the worst.

I entered a foster home at fourteen and ended

up staying for over 10 years. When I felt discouraged or depressed I would ride alone on my bike to the beach. I wanted to be alone because no one really understands how it feels to be without your family, no matter how many books they've read on the subject. Being alone to think about my family was the best medicine, next to seeing them. It gave me a chance to work things out in my own head. I stared for hours into the ocean and realized more with each crashing wave that the world and the things in it were much bigger than me. My problems didn't seem so overwhelming then.

Love and faith were, first and foremost, the crucial ingredients that set me on the right track. I learned about them from my foster parents. They made a huge difference for me. I began to realize that they really cared about me and my future. My Mom and Dad were great. I had several great teachers in high school, too. It was my foster parents, though, who really made a difference. They gave me a commitment that my success was their goal. They supported that commitment with their big hearts and strong guidance. They allowed me a safe place to live, a place I still call home more than 15 years after I first moved in. They are my nominees for sainthood.

I came to the conclusion that a lot of kids from my neighborhood were not placing any value on their future. I began seeing many of my friends falling to bad decisions with gangs, drugs and crime. Some of them died. Others went to jail. I didn't want part of either scenario. I made a decision to stop hanging out and start working harder in school. I knew I had to have the heart to set positive goals. I also knew that I needed to have the discipline necessary to achieve them. From then on, there was no holding me back.

I realized that with an education I could do anything. I focused on school, eventually receiving three college degrees: a bachelors, a masters and a law degree. It was really something for me when I got an invitation from the Lynn Tech Class of 1999 to deliver the commencement address for the graduating class. I am the first alumna in the school's history to go on to become an attorney. Since then, many students have come to me for all sorts of advice and help...some life advice and some legal advice. (Here's some free legal advice: stay out of trouble!!!)

I opened my own law office in downtown Boston, following my appointment as an Assistant District Attorney of the Eastern District of Massachusetts, in my hometown of Lynn. I was also an Assistant District Attorney for Suffolk County in Boston. I also teach graduate and undergraduate courses at Emerson College in Boston.

I am currently trying to make up for those years of missing out on my family. I am still close with my six brothers and sisters and am the pain-in-the-neck little brother they always should have had. I am also the favorite Uncle (apologies to my two brothers, Paul and Tony) of my 12 nieces and nephews. I am also Godfather to two of my nieces!

About three years ago, a friend and I founded an organization we decided to call One for the Kids. We throw a bash every year to raise money for holiday gifts and winter clothes for kids currently in foster care in Massachusetts.

Revenge is the best success! It is much more satisfying to achieve something when you've had no head start, no help and when the odds are against you.

Here's the straight dope: You can only blame how miserable you think your life is on your circumstances for just so long. Sooner or later (hopefully sooner), you have to take responsibility for what you do not have, or have not yet attained. Your successes and your failures shall equally improve the chances of future gains. Have faith in yourself and your ability to achieve great goals.

Set your sights on the impossible and the improbable. They are both imposters. Believe in your ideas and do not have fear of the unknown.

Don't be afraid to be alone; you'll be in good company. Never rest for too long. Count on yourself. Don't blame anyone but yourself, either.

Dream impossible dreams and make sure they are dreamt in living color.

Look for the doors of opportunities and knock on them nice and loud when you find them. If no one answers . . . then KNOCK THE DOORS DOWN!

And finally: never, never give up!

God bless you on your journey. If you get lost on the way (and you may get a little lost), you'll always have your inner compass.